ARABELLA BOXER

Soups

Photography by SIMON WHEELER

THE MASTER CHEFS

TED SMART

ARABELLA BOXER is half-Scottish, half-American. She lived in the north of Scotland as a child, but moved to London after the Second World War, and spent summer holidays with her American grandparents in Maine. She lived in New York, Paris and Rome before settling in London after her marriage to Mark Boxer, the cartoonist and editor.

She was food writer, and, latterly, food editor of English *Vogue* for 18 years. She has published ten books, and has won both André Simon and Glenfiddich Awards for food writing. She is currently Vice President of the Guild of Food Writers.

Photograph by Jay

CONTENTS

The mistral was still blowing, rather more softly, however, on the day I was to leave, and I had given up the idea of trying the Saint-Tropez version of soupe aux poissons; but at noon my host, an amateur cook of great skill, arrived beaming with a collection of fish and announced soupe aux poissons for lunch. I think it was the best I had ever tasted. I ate so much of it and sat at the table so late that only a sense of obligation to the family that ran the Restaurant de la Ponche where I had eaten so often took me there for an early dinner before I left. I had to say good-bye, but I had not made up my mind when I went into the place whether I would attempt to down something light or postpone the chore of eating until later – much later. But Renée, the handsome daughter of the house who waited on the clients, let out such a whoop when she saw me come in, and her mother dashed out of the kitchen wiping her hands on her apron to announce that for my last meal in Saint-Tropez she had managed to round up just enough of the right fish to make a soupe aux poissons for one (she had made enough for half a dozen). So I had another tremendous helping of the Saint-Tropez version of this dish. It is the only time in my life, I think, that I have had enough soupe aux poissons.

From *The Food of France* by Waverley Root

INTRODUCTION

It was some years before I learned to love soup. As a child, I found it hateful: thin and watery. For these were grown-up soups, based on meat. It was only after the war, in my early teens, that I started to travel and began to love soups. I was converted by the creamy vichyssoise and fish chowders of New England, the Florentine ribollita and the Parisian soupe au cresson. Now, I find soup one of the most varied and delightful of dishes.

In this book I have chosen a few of my favourites, with garnishes to make them even more appealing. (The garnishes may be omitted if time is short.) They range from elegant game consommé with chervil dumplings to homely cabbage soup with croûtes; from warming curried leek soup with saffron, to chilled aubergine, pepper and tomato soup. All are easy to make, colourful and full of interest.

Arabella Boxer.

GRILLED AUBERGINE SOUP
with peppers and tomatoes

1 LARGE AUBERGINE

2 RED PEPPERS

3 TABLESPOONS SUNFLOWER OIL

1 BUNCH OF SPRING ONIONS,
SLICED

3 BEEFSTEAK TOMATOES, SKINNED
AND CUT INTO QUARTERS

500 ML/16 FL OZ CHICKEN STOCK
(PAGE 29)

2 TABLESPOONS FRESH ORANGE
JUICE

2 TABLESPOONS FRESH LIME JUICE

SEA SALT AND BLACK PEPPER

1½ TABLESPOONS CHOPPED FRESH
CORIANDER

SERVES 6

Grill the aubergine and peppers under a hot grill, turning frequently, until the peppers are charred evenly all over, about 12 minutes. Remove the peppers, leaving the aubergine under the grill for a further 12–15 minutes or until soft when squeezed.

Leave the peppers and aubergines until they are cool enough to handle. Skin the peppers, discarding the interior membrane and seeds, and chop roughly. Cut the aubergine in half lengthways, scoop out the flesh with a spoon and chop roughly.

Heat the oil in a small frying pan and cook the sliced spring onions for 3 minutes.

Put the tomatoes into a liquidizer or food processor and process to a rough pulp. Add the chopped peppers and aubergine and process again. Add the spring onions, chicken stock, orange and lime juice, salt and pepper and process once more. Chill for at least 1 hour.

Serve sprinkled with coriander.

BLACK BEAN SOUP
with Bourbon

325 G/12 OZ DRIED BLACK BEANS
1 RED ONION, SLICED
3 WHOLE GARLIC CLOVES
1 BAY LEAF
3 CLOVES
3 TABLESPOONS SUNFLOWER OIL
1 LEEK, FINELY CHOPPED
3 FRESH RED CHILLIES, SEEDED AND
    FINELY CHOPPED
1 TABLESPOON GROUND CUMIN
1 TABLESPOON GROUND
    CORIANDER
300–600 ML/½–1 PINT CHICKEN
    STOCK (PAGE 29)
SEA SALT AND BLACK PEPPER
¼ TEASPOON CAYENNE PEPPER
JUICE OF 2 LIMES OR 1 LEMON

GARNISH

3–4 TABLESPOONS BOURBON
    WHISKEY (OPTIONAL)
300 ML/½ PINT FROMAGE FRAIS
SALSA FRESCA (PAGE 30)
4 TABLESPOONS COARSELY
    CHOPPED FRESH CORIANDER

SERVES 6

Soak the beans in cold water
overnight. Drain and place in a
saucepan with 1.5 litres/2½ pints
cold water, the onion, garlic, bay
leaf and cloves. Bring to the boil
and boil fast for 10 minutes, then
lower the heat and simmer gently
for about 1 hour or until the beans
are tender.

Lift out 225 g/8 oz of the beans
and reserve. Discard the bay leaf.
Purée the remaining beans and
cooking liquid in a food processor.

Heat the oil in a large saucepan
and cook the leek for 3 minutes.
Add the chillies, cumin and ground
coriander and cook for a further 3
minutes, stirring frequently. Add
300 ml/½ pint of the stock, with
salt, pepper and cayenne to taste.
Simmer for 20 minutes, then add
the whole and puréed beans and
simmer for a further 15 minutes.

Thin the soup with more stock,
if needed, and add the lime juice.

Serve hot, with ½ tablespoon
bourbon in each bowl, for those
who like it. Serve the fromage
frais, Salsa Fresca and chopped
coriander in separate bowls.

CABBAGE SOUP WITH CROÛTES

600 ML/1 PINT CHICKEN STOCK
  (PAGE 29)
675 G/1½ LB CABBAGE (WEIGHED
  AFTER TRIMMING), THICKLY
  SLICED
40 G/1½ OZ BUTTER
1 TABLESPOON SUNFLOWER OIL
2 ONIONS, CHOPPED
1 LARGE POTATO, SLICED
SEA SALT AND BLACK PEPPER
300 ML/½ PINT MILK

GARNISH

6 SLICES OF DAY-OLD COUNTRY
  BREAD, ABOUT 1 CM/½ INCH
  THICK, HALVED IF LARGE
25 G/1 OZ BUTTER

SERVES 6

Put the stock into a large saucepan, add the cabbage, bring to the boil, then simmer for 6 minutes. Drain, reserving the stock.

In a clean pan, heat the butter and oil and fry the onion gently for 10 minutes. Add the sliced potato and cook for a further 3 minutes. Pour on the hot cabbage stock and simmer for 25 minutes.

Add the cooked cabbage and 600 ml/1 pint water. Bring back to the boil and simmer for 10 minutes. Season to taste with salt and pepper.

Leave to cool for 5 minutes, then lift out about 325 g/12 oz of the cooked cabbage. Process or chop this cabbage and keep warm. Pour the rest of the soup into a liquidizer or food processor and blend with the milk. Reheat and adjust the seasoning to taste.

To serve, toast the bread and spread lightly with butter. Pile the chopped cabbage on the croûtes, allowing about 2 tablespoons for each one. Serve the soup hot, in broad soup plates or bowls, with a croûte in each.

CORN SOUP
with cherry tomatoes

4 EARS OF SWEETCORN, OR
400 G/14 OZ FROZEN
SWEETCORN KERNELS
1 LITRE/1¾ PINTS LIGHT CHICKEN
STOCK (PAGE 29)
25 G/1 OZ BUTTER
1 TABLESPOON SUNFLOWER OIL
2 BUNCHES OF SPRING ONIONS,
WHITE PARTS ONLY, SLICED
SEA SALT AND BLACK PEPPER
¼ TEASPOON DRIED CHILLI FLAKES
(OPTIONAL)

GARNISH

6 CHERRY TOMATOES, CUT INTO
3–4 THICK SLICES
1 TABLESPOON OLIVE OIL

SERVES 6

Slice the kernels off the ears of corn, using a small sharp knife. Bring the stock to the boil and set aside.

Heat the butter and oil in a large saucepan over low heat and cook the sliced spring onions for 3 minutes, then add the corn kernels. Cook gently for 3 minutes, then pour on the hot stock, adding salt, pepper and chilli flakes to taste. Bring to the boil, then simmer gently, half covered, for 15 minutes, or 10 minutes if using frozen corn.

Leave to cool slightly, then purée in a liquidizer or food processor. Return to the pan to reheat; adjust the seasoning to taste.

Brush the cherry tomato slices with olive oil and quickly brown in a nonstick pan over high heat. Pour the soup into individual bowls and serve hot, garnished with the tomato slices.

Alternatively, omit the chilli flakes when cooking the soup and omit the tomato garnish; instead add a spoonful of cold Salsa Fresca (page 30) to each bowl of hot soup.

MEDITERRANEAN FISH SOUP
with rouille

900 G/2 LB MIXED FISH (GREY
    MULLET, MONKFISH, COD,
    CONGER EEL), FILLETED
25 G/1 OZ BUTTER
1½ TABLESPOONS OLIVE OIL
3 SHALLOTS, CHOPPED
1 LEEK, WHITE PART ONLY,
    CHOPPED
1 STICK OF CELERY, CHOPPED
1 CARROT, CHOPPED
2 GARLIC CLOVES, CHOPPED
2 TOMATOES, CHOPPED
SEA SALT AND BLACK PEPPER
1 TEASPOON MILD CURRY POWDER
85 ML/3 FL OZ DRY VERMOUTH
1 SMALL BAY LEAF
1 SPRIG OF THYME

GARNISH

6 SLICES OF DAY-OLD FRENCH
    BREAD, ABOUT 1 CM/½ INCH
    THICK
ROUILLE (PAGE 29)
FRESHLY GRATED PARMESAN
    CHEESE

SERVES 6

Cut the fish into chunks. Heat the butter and oil in a large saucepan and cook the shallots for 3 minutes, then add the leek, celery, carrot, garlic and tomatoes. Cook for a further 3 minutes, then add the pieces of fish, salt, pepper and curry powder. Stir for 2–3 minutes, then pour on the vermouth and 1.2 litres/2 pints hot water. Add the herbs and bring to the boil, then simmer for 1 hour, with the pan half covered.

Meanwhile, heat the oven to 150°C/300°F/Gas Mark 2 and put the bread in to dry out for 20 minutes or until lightly coloured.

Leave the soup to cool slightly, then purée in a liquidizer or food processor and rub through a coarse sieve – leave unsieved if you prefer.

Serve hot, accompanied by the bread, Rouille and grated Parmesan in separate bowls, for guests to help themselves.

THAI FISH SOUP
with tiger prawns

1.2 LITRES/2 PINTS LIGHT CHICKEN
STOCK (PAGE 29)

325 G/12 OZ TIGER PRAWNS, OR
OTHER GIANT PRAWNS IN THEIR
SHELLS, UNCOOKED

1 GREEN CHILLI

2 LEMONGRASS STALKS, PEELED AND
CRUSHED

2.5 CM/1 INCH PIECE OF FRESH
GINGER, SLICED AND CRUSHED

85 G/3 OZ MANGETOUTS

1 FRESH RED CHILLI, SEEDED AND
THINLY SLICED IN RINGS

3 TABLESPOONS FRESH LIME OR
LEMON JUICE

2 TABLESPOONS ROUGHLY TORN
CORIANDER LEAVES

SERVES 6

Put the stock into a saucepan. Shell the prawns and drop the heads and shells into the stock. Heat slowly, adding the whole green chilli, lemongrass and ginger. When it reaches boiling point, half-cover the saucepan and simmer gently for 20 minutes.

Split open the mangetouts, reserve any peas inside, and cut the pods lengthways into thin shreds.

Pour the soup through a muslin-lined sieve into a clean pan and bring back to the boil. Add the shelled prawns and the sliced red chilli and poach gently for 3 minutes, then add the shredded mangetouts and cook for a further 3 minutes. Remove from the heat, add the tiny shelled peas and leave to cool.

After 10 minutes, stir in the lime or lemon juice. Divide the prawns between six bowls and spoon the soup over them. Scatter a few torn coriander leaves over each bowl and serve at once.

GAME CONSOMMÉ
with chervil dumplings

1 PHEASANT, OR 2 PHEASANT
CARCASSES

6 GARLIC CLOVES, ROUGHLY
CRUSHED

6 LEMONGRASS STALKS, PEELED AND
ROUGHLY CRUSHED

25 G/1 OZ FRESH GINGER, SLICED
AND ROUGHLY CRUSHED

8 BLACK PEPPERCORNS, ROUGHLY
CRUSHED

1.2 LITRES/2 PINTS LIGHT CHICKEN
STOCK (PAGE 29)

½ TABLESPOON SEA SALT

CHERVIL DUMPLINGS (PAGE 30)

SERVES 6

Begin making the consommé the day before you want to serve it. Put the bird, or carcasses, into a large saucepan and add the garlic, lemongrass, ginger and peppercorns. Add the stock and bring very slowly to the boil, skimming frequently as it nears boiling point. Once the surface is clear, half-cover the pan and simmer for 2½ hours (or cook for 50 minutes in a pressure cooker.) If using a raw bird, remove it after 1 hour (or 20 minutes in a pressure cooker) and remove the breast fillets, then return the bird to the pan. When the full time is up, strain the stock into a bowl. Leave to cool, then chill overnight.

The next day, remove all fat from the surface of the stock. If using a whole bird, cut the reserved breast meat into neat dice, discarding the skin.

Shortly before serving, make the Chervil Dumplings. Reheat the soup with the diced breast meat and adjust the seasoning to taste. Serve hot, with 2–3 dumplings in each bowl.

CURRIED LEEK SOUP
with saffron

450 G /1 LB LEEKS, WHITE PARTS
 ONLY, WEIGHED AFTER
 TRIMMING
50 G/2 OZ BUTTER
1 TABLESPOON SUNFLOWER OIL
2 TABLESPOONS FLOUR
1 TABLESPOON MILD CURRY
 POWDER
1 LITRE/1¾ PINTS LIGHT CHICKEN
 STOCK (PAGE 29)

GARNISH

½ TEASPOON SAFFRON STRANDS
1½ TABLESPOONS SUNFLOWER OIL
1 LEEK, WHITE PART ONLY, THINLY
 SLICED
85 ML/3 FL OZ SINGLE CREAM

SERVES 6

Slice the leeks. Heat the butter and oil in a large saucepan, add the leeks and cook gently for at least 10 minutes, allowing them to soften but without letting them brown. Add the flour and curry powder and cook gently for 3 minutes, stirring frequently. Heat the stock, add to the pan and bring to the boil, stirring, then lower the heat and simmer for 15 minutes.

Leave to cool slightly, then purée the soup in a liquidizer or food processor and return to the cleaned pan.

Shortly before serving, make the garnish. Warm the saffron in a large metal spoon over a low heat for about 30 seconds. Pound it in a mortar, pour on 1 tablespoon boiling water and leave to infuse. Heat the oil in a small frying pan and fry the sliced leek for 2 minutes, then add the saffron and cook for a further 1 minute, stirring constantly.

Reheat the soup and pour into bowls. Drizzle 1 tablespoon cream over each bowl and scatter some saffron leek rings over the top.

LENTIL BROTH
with crispy duck skin

25 G/1 OZ BUTTER

2 TABLESPOONS OLIVE OIL

1 LEEK, THINLY SLICED

1 SMALL CARROT, SLICED

1 SMALL STICK OF CELERY, SLICED

225 G/8 OZ PUY LENTILS, WASHED
AND DRAINED

BROTH

½ DUCK

1 LEEK, HALVED

1 CARROT, HALVED

1 STICK OF CELERY, HALVED

1 BAY LEAF

150 ML/¼ PINT DRY WHITE WINE

1 LITRE/1¾ PINTS LIGHT CHICKEN
STOCK (PAGE 29)

SEA SALT AND BLACK PEPPER

SERVES 6

Begin making the broth the day before you want to serve it. Cut the breast meat off the duck; detach the skin and set aside. Put the carcass into a saucepan with the broth ingredients. Bring to the boil and simmer for 2½ hours. Strain, cool and chill overnight.

The next day, remove all fat from the surface and reheat the broth. Heat the butter and oil in a large saucepan and cook the sliced leek for 2 minutes. Add the carrot and celery and cook for 2 minutes. Add the drained lentils, stir for 1 minute, then pour on the hot broth and simmer for 20 minutes. Adjust the seasoning to taste, add the whole duck breast and poach gently for 15 minutes.

Meanwhile, remove most of the fat from the duck skin; cut the skin into strips. Fry gently in a nonstick pan for about 4 minutes or until they have become crisp and golden brown. Drain on paper towels.

Cut the poached duck breast into dice. Serve the soup hot, with some of the diced breast in each bowl, sprinkled with the crisp skin.

RUBY RED CONSOMMÉ

675 G/1½ LB SHIN OF BEEF, CUBED

SOME BEEF OR VEAL BONES (E.G.
    KNUCKLE OF VEAL)

1 ONION, HALVED

1 LEEK, HALVED

1 CARROT, HALVED

1 STICK OF CELERY, HALVED

3 PARSLEY STALKS

1 BAY LEAF

10 BLACK PEPPERCORNS

SEA SALT AND BLACK PEPPER

225 G/8 OZ BEETROOT, RAW OR
    COOKED, SKINNED AND
    COARSELY GRATED

3 TABLESPOONS LEMON JUICE

SERVES 6

Begin making the consommé the day before you want to serve it. Put the beef and bones into a pressure cooker or deep saucepan. Add 1.7 litres/3 pints cold water and bring very slowly to the boil. As it nears boiling point, skim frequently until the surface is clear. Then add 150 ml/¼ pint cold water, the onion, leek, carrot, celery, parsley, bay leaf and peppercorns. Cover and simmer for 1 hour under pressure, or 3 hours in an ordinary pan. Strain and leave to cool, then chill overnight.

The next day, remove all fat from the surface of the stock; you should be left with about 1.5 litres/2½ pints of stock. Bring back to the boil, adding sea salt and black pepper to taste. Measure 300 ml/½ pint of the boiling stock, pour it over the grated beetroot and leave for 30 minutes.

Strain the red stock back into the consommé. Reheat and add the lemon juice. Serve hot, or chilled, in bowls.

THE BASICS

VEGETABLE STOCK

3 ONIONS, INCLUDING SKINS,
   ROUGHLY CHOPPED
3 LEEKS, ROUGHLY CHOPPED
3 CARROTS, ROUGHLY CHOPPED
2 STICKS OF CELERY, ROUGHLY
   CHOPPED
1 FENNEL BULB, ROUGHLY CHOPPED
225 G/8 OZ SPINACH, ROUGHLY
   CHOPPED
225 G/8 OZ TOMATOES, ROUGHLY
   CHOPPED
½ TABLESPOON SEA SALT

Put all the vegetables except the spinach and tomatoes in a pressure cooker or deep saucepan. Add 1.5 litres/2½ pints cold water and the salt. Bring slowly to the boil, then simmer for 20 minutes under pressure, or 1 hour in an ordinary saucepan.

If using a pressure cooker, leave to cool briefly, then add the spinach and tomatoes, and cook for a further 10 minutes under pressure. (Alternatively, cook for a further 30 minutes in an ordinary pan.) Strain, cool and adjust the seasoning to taste.

This makes about 1.5 litres/ 2½ pints of light stock, which may be reduced by fast boiling to concentrate the flavour.

CHICKEN STOCK

675 G/1½ LB CHICKEN WINGS, OR
   1 CHICKEN CARCASS
1 LARGE ONION, QUARTERED
2 LEEKS, ROUGHLY CHOPPED
2 CARROTS, ROUGHLY CHOPPED
2 STICKS OF CELERY, ROUGHLY
   CHOPPED
1 BAY LEAF
½ TABLESPOON SEA SALT
12 BLACK PEPPERCORNS

Put all the ingredients into a pressure cooker or deep saucepan. Add 1 litre/1¾ pints water. Bring slowly to the boil, then cook for 1 hour under pressure, or 3 hours in an ordinary pan. Strain and cool, then chill overnight.

The next day, remove all fat from the surface. This will give you about 900 ml/1½ pints of well-flavoured stock, which can be diluted to make 1.2 litres/2 pints.

ROUILLE

50 G/2 OZ DAY-OLD WHITE BREAD,
   CRUSTS REMOVED
6 TABLESPOONS MILK
¼ TEASPOON SAFFRON STRANDS
1 TABLESPOON FISH STOCK, HOT
3 RED CHILLIES, FRESH OR DRIED,
   SPLIT, SEEDED AND CHOPPED
3 GARLIC CLOVES, FINELY CHOPPED
¼ TEASPOON SEA SALT
4 TABLESPOONS EXTRA VIRGIN
   OLIVE OIL
2 TABLESPOONS FISH SOUP
   (PAGE 16)

Soak the bread in the milk for 10 minutes, then squeeze dry. Warm the saffron in a metal spoon over a low heat for about 30 seconds, then pound it in a mortar. Pour over the hot fish stock and leave to infuse. Pound the chillies, garlic and salt in a mortar, then add the soaked bread and continue pounding. When all is amalgamated, start to pour in the olive oil very slowly, as if making mayonnaise, continuing to pound until all is blended. Finally, stir in 2 tablespoons of fish soup. Serve the rouille spread on bread croûtons, with the fish soup, or separately, in a small bowl.

CHERVIL DUMPLINGS

40 G/1½ OZ BUTTER, SOFTENED
1 EGG, BEATEN
PINCH OF SALT
50 G/2 OZ SOFT WHITE
  BREADCRUMBS
2 TABLESPOONS FINELY CHOPPED
  CHERVIL

Beat the softened butter with a wooden spoon, then gradually add the beaten egg, beating constantly. Add the salt, breadcrumbs and chopped chervil, beating until thoroughly blended. Cover and leave for 30 minutes.

Form the mixture into tiny balls, not much bigger than your thumbnail; you should make about 18 dumplings. Drop them into a wide pan of lightly salted simmering water and cook gently for 5 minutes. Have the hot soup already in bowls, then put 2–3 dumplings into each bowl.

SALSA FRESCA

4 RIPE TOMATOES, CUT INTO
  CHUNKS
1 LARGE GARLIC CLOVE, FINELY
  CHOPPED
1 FRESH RED CHILLI, SEEDED AND
  FINELY CHOPPED
1½ TABLESPOONS FRESH LIME JUICE
1½ TABLESPOONS CHOPPED FRESH
  CORIANDER

Put the tomato chunks into a food processor with the garlic and chilli. Process to a rough purée, then add the lime juice and coriander and process again briefly.

Serve as an optional garnish to Corn Soup or Black Bean Soup, either adding 1 tablespoon cold Salsa Fresca to each bowl, or serving separately, in a bowl.

THE MASTER CHEFS

SOUPS
ARABELLA BOXER

MEZE, TAPAS AND ANTIPASTI
AGLAIA KREMEZI

PASTA SAUCES
GORDON RAMSAY

RISOTTO
MICHELE SCICOLONE

SALADS
CLARE CONNERY

MEDITERRANEAN
ANTONY WORRALL THOMPSON

VEGETABLES
PAUL GAYLER

LUNCHES
ALASTAIR LITTLE

COOKING FOR TWO
RICHARD OLNEY

FISH
RICK STEIN

CHICKEN
BRUNO LOUBET

SUPPERS
VALENTINA HARRIS

THE MAIN COURSE
ROGER VERGÉ

ROASTS
JANEEN SARLIN

WILD FOOD
ROWLEY LEIGH

PACIFIC
JILL DUPLEIX

CURRIES
PAT CHAPMAN

HOT AND SPICY
PAUL AND JEANNE RANKIN

THAI
JACKI PASSMORE

CHINESE
YAN-KIT SO

VEGETARIAN
KAREN LEE

DESSERTS
MICHEL ROUX

CAKES
CAROLE WALTER

COOKIES
ELINOR KLIVANS

THE MASTER CHEFS

This edition produced for The Book People Ltd,

Hall Wood Avenue, Haydock, St Helens WAII 9UL

First published in 1996 by
WEIDENFELD & NICOLSON
THE ORION PUBLISHING GROUP
ORION HOUSE
5 UPPER ST MARTIN'S LANE
LONDON WC2H 9EA

British Library Cataloguing-in-Publication data
A catalogue record for this book is available from the British Library.

ISBN 0 297 83611 0

DESIGNED BY THE SENATE
EDITOR MAGGIE RAMSAY
FOOD STYLIST JOY DAVIES
ASSISTANT KATY HOLDER

ACKNOWLEDGEMENT
Excerpt (page 6) from *The Food of France* by Waverley Root
Copyright © 1958, 1966 by Waverley Root
Reprinted by permission of Alfred A Knopf Inc.